I didn't know that
some
cars can swim

© Aladdin Books Ltd 1999
Produced by
Aladdin Books Ltd
28 Percy Street
London W1P 0LD

First published in the United States in 1999 by
Copper Beech Books,
an imprint of
The Millbrook Press
2 Old New Milford Road
Brookfield, Connecticut 06804

Concept, editorial and design by
David West Children's Books

Designer: Simon Morse

Illustrators: Gerald Witcomb and Don Simpson – Specs Art,
Jo Moore

Library of Congress Cataloging-in-Publication Data
Petty, William. 1979-
Some cars can swim / William Petty.
p. cm. – (I didn't know that –)
Includes index.
Summary: Explores the world of cars throughout history, examining
the ways cars are built, how they work, and what kinds are available today.
ISBN 0-7613-0921-7 (lib. bdg.)
ISNB 0-7613-0798-2 (trade hc)
1. Automobiles Miscellanea Juvenile literature.
[1. Automobiles Miscellanea.] I. Title. II. Series.
TL206.P48 1999   99-39174
629.222–dc21   CIP

Printed in Belgium

5 4 3 2 1

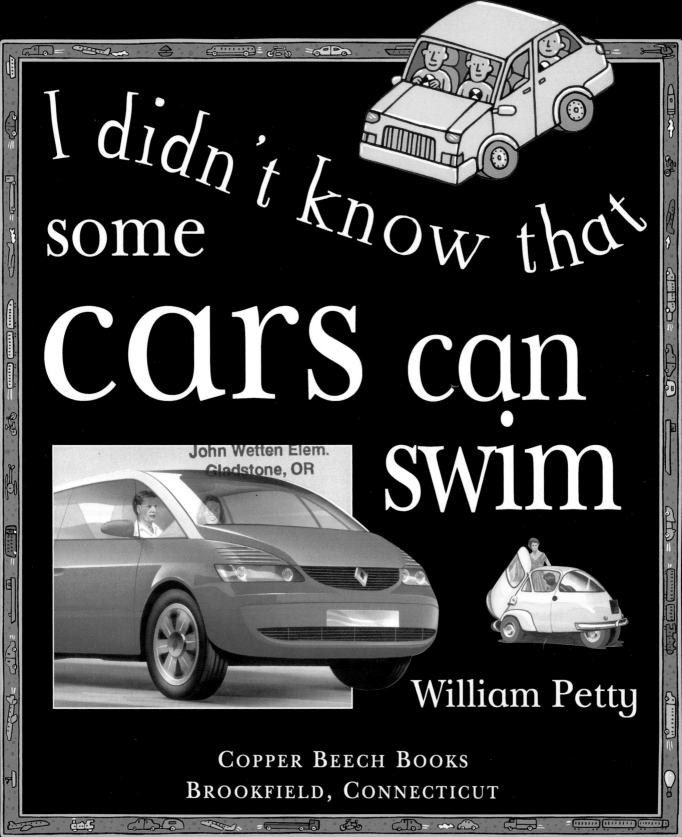

I didn't know that
some
cars can
swim

John Wetten Elem.
Gladstone, OR

William Petty

COPPER BEECH BOOKS
BROOKFIELD, CONNECTICUT

I didn't know that

Introduction

Did *you* know that some cars have wings? ... that some cars have two engines? ... that Formula One pit-crews can change tires in seconds?

Discover for yourself amazing facts about cars, from the very earliest models with three wheels to today's record breakers that go faster than the speed of sound.

Watch for this symbol that means there is a fun project for you to try.

Is it true or is it false? Watch for this symbol and try to answer the question before reading on for the answer.

I didn't know that

the first cars had three wheels. The first successful car was the Benz Motorwagen. It had three wheels, a *gasoline engine* and a top speed of 20 miles per hour.

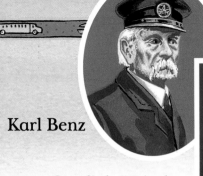

Karl Benz

Gottlieb Daimler

Karl Benz and Gottlieb Daimler both worked separately to develop petrol engines. Their names are still familiar today.

The Bordino Steam Carriage of 1854 replaced horses with steam power. It was very heavy and cumbersome, and slower than traveling by train. Cars soon became popular and replaced these "horseless carriages."

True or false?
Early cars had no speed limit.

Answer: **False**

The 1865 British law said that cars must follow a man with a red flag at less than 4 miles per hour.

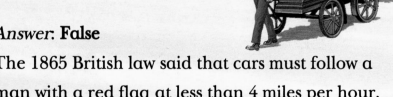

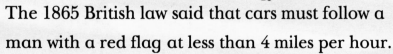

Because early cars were open, coats and hats were essential.

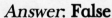
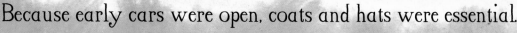

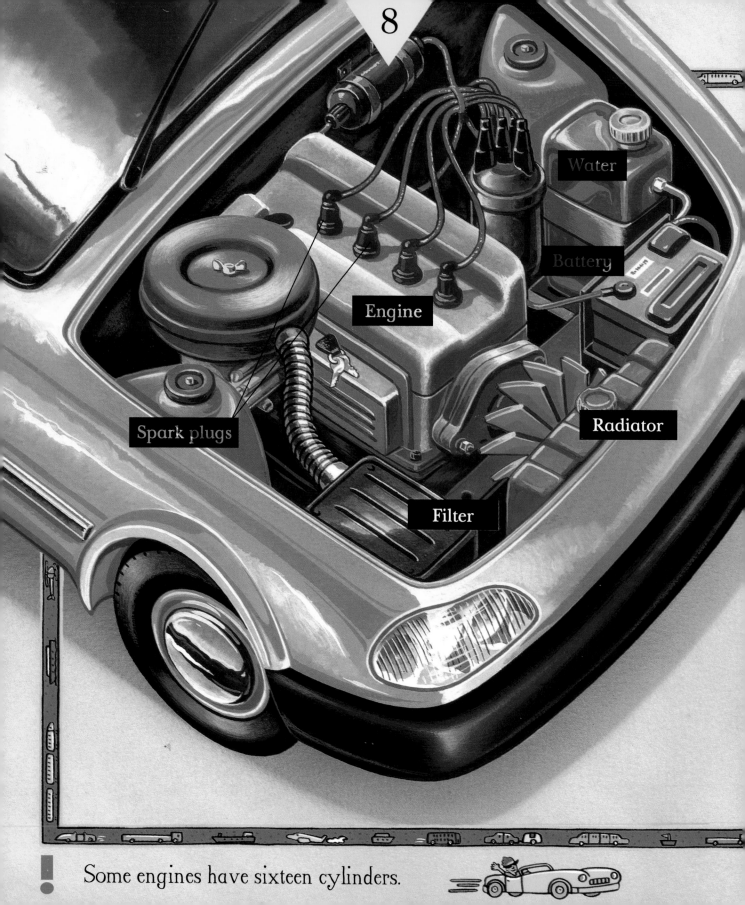

Water

Battery

Engine

Spark plugs

Radiator

Filter

Some engines have sixteen cylinders.

Can you find the car keys?

SEARCH & FIND & SEARCH & FIND &

I didn't know that

cars are powered by explosions. Inside a car's engine gasoline mixed with air is exploded. This force pushes the pistons, driving the engine.

True or false?
All cars have engines under the hood.

Answer: **False**
Some, such as the Volkswagen Beetle and the Fiat Seicento, have the engine in the trunk! Under the hood there is space for luggage.

The spark plugs create the sparks that ignite the mixture of gasoline and air in the engine. The battery starts the engine and supplies power to other electrical systems. Air for the engine is cleaned by a filter and water cools the engine using the radiator.

9

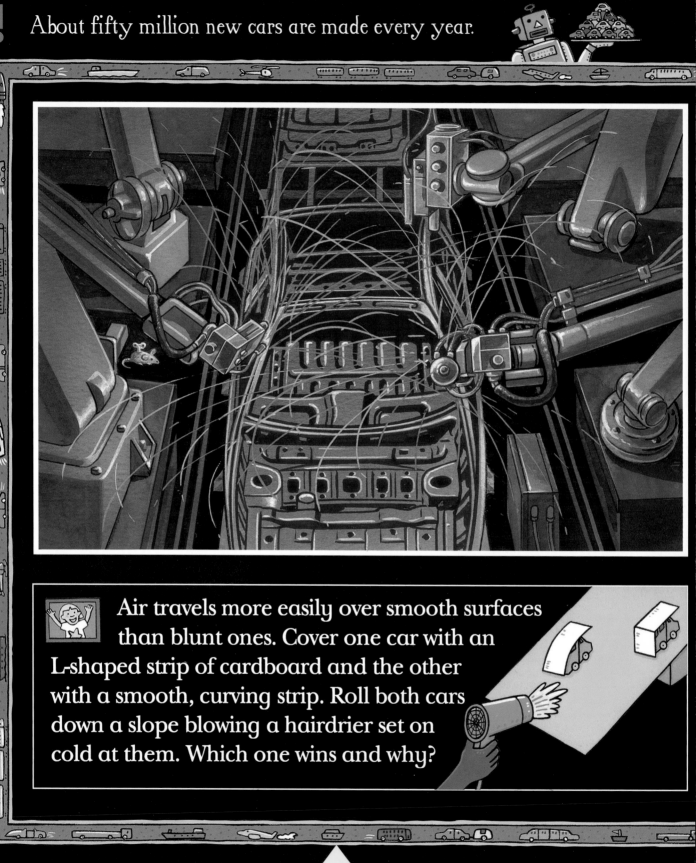

Air travels more easily over smooth surfaces than blunt ones. Cover one car with an L-shaped strip of cardboard and the other with a smooth, curving strip. Roll both cars down a slope blowing a hairdrier set on cold at them. Which one wins and why?

SEARCH & FIND & FIND & SEARCH &

Can you find the clockwork mouse?

I didn't know that

robots build cars. Modern cars are built quickly and accurately by robots, each with its own task. Robots can work in conditions that are too hot, noisy, or dangerous for humans.

Today, modern cars are designed using computers. Designers can see easily what the finished car will look like. Then a life-size model of the car is tested for *aerodynamic* properties in a wind tunnel.

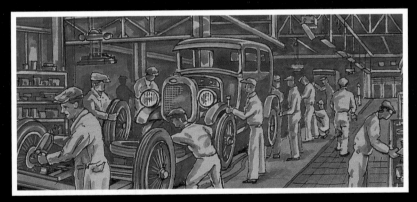

The Model-T Ford was the world's first-ever *mass-produced* car. Henry Ford invented the *production line* for building cars in 1913.

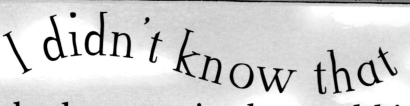

I didn't know that

the best car in the world is a ghost.
The Rolls Royce Silver Ghost was renowned for its superb engine and stylish looks. Some people consider it to be the best car in the world.

The stylish 1935 Auburn Speedster was perfect for cruising around glamourous Hollywood.
Each car came with a plaque certifying that it had been driven at over 99 miles per hour by racing driver Ab Jenkins.

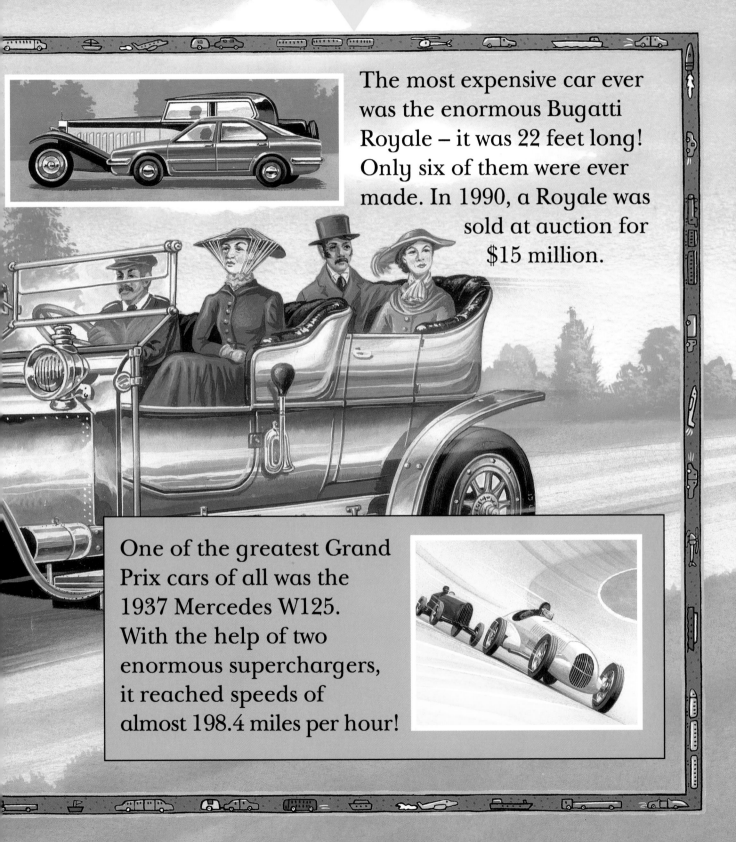

The most expensive car ever was the enormous Bugatti Royale – it was 22 feet long! Only six of them were ever made. In 1990, a Royale was sold at auction for $15 million.

One of the greatest Grand Prix cars of all was the 1937 Mercedes W125. With the help of two enormous superchargers, it reached speeds of almost 198.4 miles per hour!

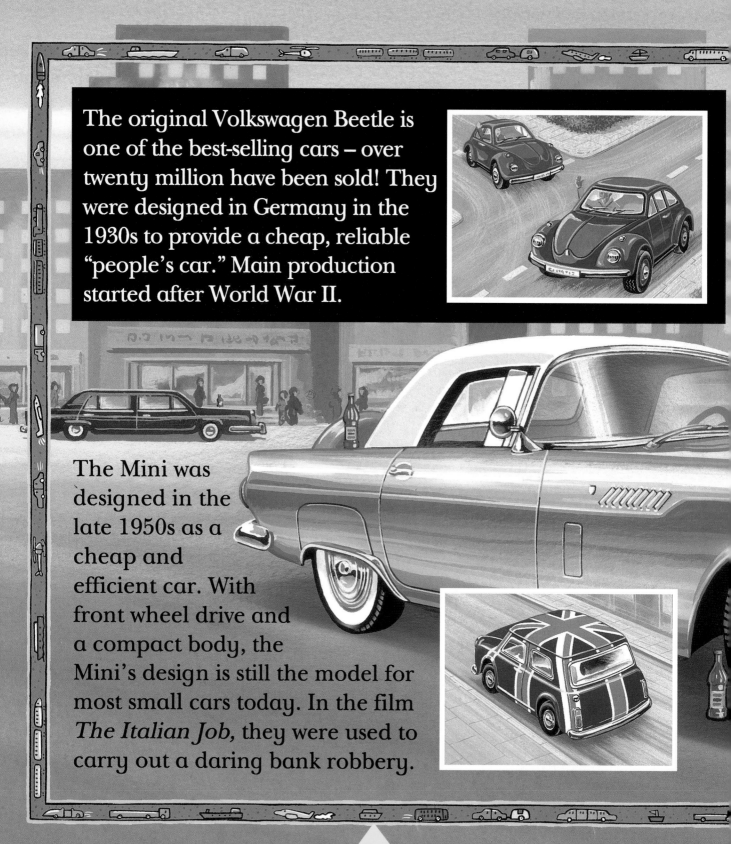

The original Volkswagen Beetle is one of the best-selling cars – over twenty million have been sold! They were designed in Germany in the 1930s to provide a cheap, reliable "people's car." Main production started after World War II.

The Mini was designed in the late 1950s as a cheap and efficient car. With front wheel drive and a compact body, the Mini's design is still the model for most small cars today. In the film *The Italian Job*, they were used to carry out a daring bank robbery.

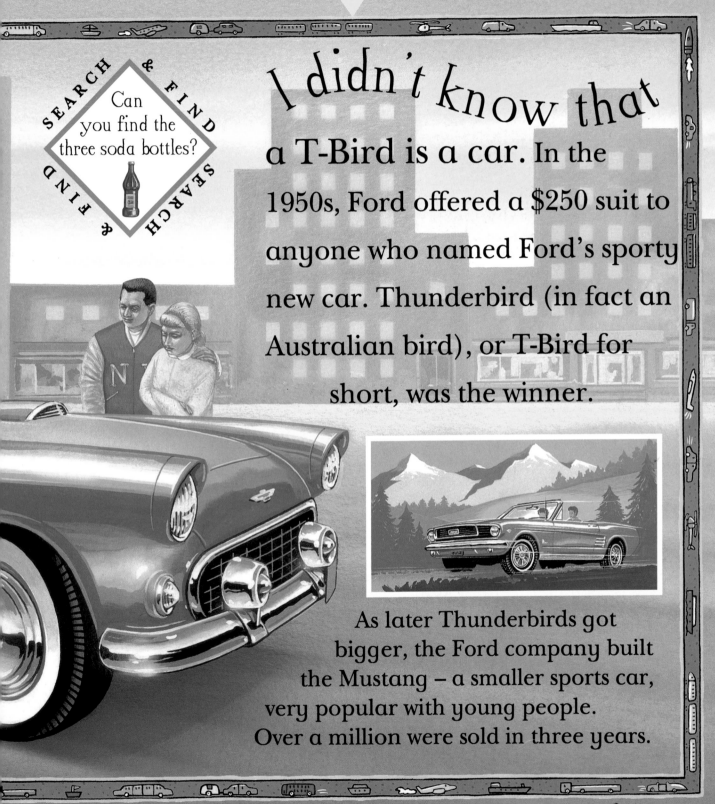

Can you find the three soda bottles?

SEARCH & FIND & SEARCH & FIND &

I didn't know that a T-Bird is a car. In the 1950s, Ford offered a $250 suit to anyone who named Ford's sporty new car. Thunderbird (in fact an Australian bird), or T-Bird for short, was the winner.

As later Thunderbirds got bigger, the Ford company built the Mustang – a smaller sports car, very popular with young people. Over a million were sold in three years.

In 1972, forty-six Australian students got in one Mini!

I didn't know that

dummies test cars. New cars undergo a series of safety tests. Dummies, accurate models of humans, are used to see how the car behaves in a series of crash situations.

SEARCH & FIND
Can you find the crash test bear?
FIND & SEARCH

Early brakes often failed.

Many different kinds of crashes are simulated. Cars have to protect passengers from front and side impacts. *Airbags* (right) in the front and sides are fully tested.

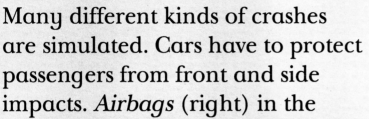

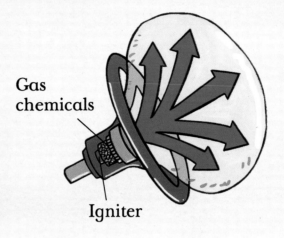

Gas chemicals

Igniter

Chemicals will inflate an airbag in forty milliseconds. This is less than a third of the time it takes to blink!

 True or false?
Some cars are armor-plated.

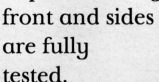

Answer: **True**
This Zil limousine, used by Russian presidents, could

be the safest car in the world! It weighs 6.6 tons and is covered with 3-inch-thick steel armor plating.

John Wetten Elem.
Gladstone, OR

The first Grand Prix race ("big prize" in French) was in France in 1906.

Every year, drivers compete in up to sixteen Formula One Grand Prix races around the world. Each race is at least 186 miles long. Monaco is a difficult race, where drivers have to negotiate narrow city streets at high speed.

Formula One cars need to have different types of tires for wet and dry weather. Normally the tires are changed mid-race.

Racing tire

Wet-weather tire

I didn't know that

some cars have wings. *Formula One* cars go at above 186 miles per hour and are designed with upside-down wings, which push the car downward. This helps them to grip the track.

True or false?
You can change tires in seconds.

Answer: **True**
During a race drivers can pull into the pit-lane to change tires, re-fuel or for minor repairs. Pit-crew mechanics are trained to change tires and add fuel in seconds.

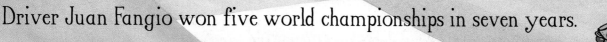

! Driver Juan Fangio won five world championships in seven years.

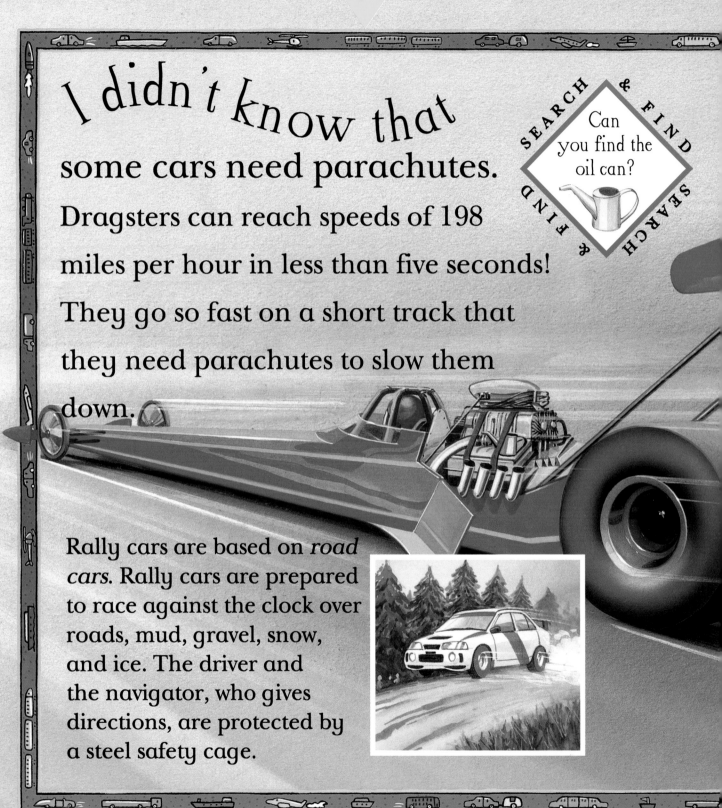

I didn't know that

some cars need parachutes.

Dragsters can reach speeds of 198 miles per hour in less than five seconds! They go so fast on a short track that they need parachutes to slow them down.

SEARCH & FIND
Can you find the oil can?
FIND & SEARCH

Rally cars are based on *road cars*. Rally cars are prepared to race against the clock over roads, mud, gravel, snow, and ice. The driver and the navigator, who gives directions, are protected by a steel safety cage.

The longest-ever rally is from London to Sydney - 19,131.3 miles!

At Le Mans, cars race for 24 hours only stopping to change drivers, re-fuel or have minor repairs. The race used to begin with drivers running to their cars, but this was abandoned because it was too dangerous.

To see how a parachute will help to slow down a speeding car, attach a piece of string to each corner of a hankie. Fasten the ends of the strings to a ball of clay. Throw it high into the air.

Not all record-breakers look so sleek. The odd-looking, pancake-shaped *Napier Railton* was also a record breaker. Driven by John Cobb in 1947, it reached a speed of 391 miles per hour.

The 223-miles-per-hour *McLaren F-1* is the fastest road car ever. Underneath it has fans that "glue" it to the road.

I didn't know that

a car can go faster than sound. In October 1997, *Thrust SCC* became the first car to break the *sound barrier*. In Black Rock, Nevada, it reached an incredible 764.8 miles per hour!

Donald Campbell broke the land-speed record in 1964, reaching speeds of 430 miles per hour in his gas-powered *Bluebird* car.

In 1994 an electric car traveled at 186 miles per hour.

I didn't know that

some cars can swim. The Lotus Esprit in the James Bond film *The Spy Who Loved Me* could change into a submarine. Under water, propellers took over.

This funny-looking car is the 1923 Leyat Aerocar. It was pulled along by an enormous wooden propeller at up to 99 miles per hour. However, propeller cars never became popular.

SEARCH & FIND
Can you find the starfish?
FIND & SEARCH

The world's smallest model car is only 0.31 inches long.

John Wetten Elem.
Gladstone, OR

Cars that regularly drive off the road, like the Range Rover, need to have large, chunky tires and specially-strengthened and raised *suspension* to avoid getting stuck in the mud. It can drive over rough country, across ice, and through small rivers.

The Bubble car was briefly popular in the 1950s as a small car for city dwellers. It had a 2-cylinder engine, a door at the front, three wheels, and no reverse gear.

I didn't know that

some cars have two engines.

The Toyota Prius has an *electric engine* for low speeds, and a gasoline engine that kicks in when the car reaches a higher speed.

SEARCH & FIND
Can you find five rabbits?
FIND & SEARCH

26

This car has been fitted with a *solar panel* on the roof that absorbs heat energy from the sun and converts it into electricity. Cars like this need a hot climate. In Australia, there is a race from Darwin to Adelaide that is exclusively for solar-powered cars.

Some cars are entirely driven by electric motors. They are better for the environment, but they are expensive to run and have a very short range.

! Some London taxis in 1896 were electric powered.

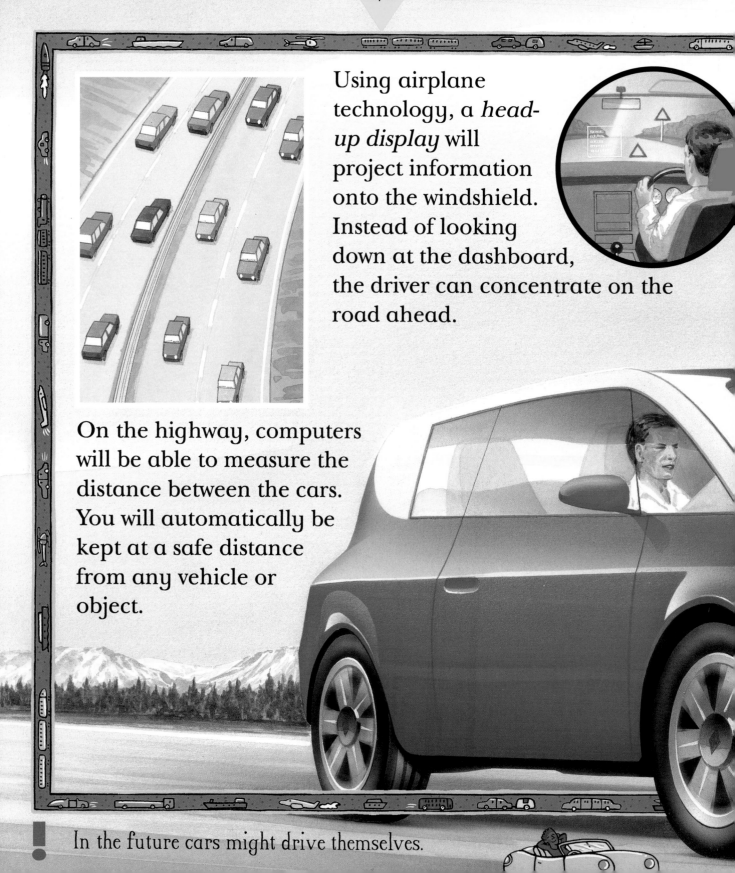

Using airplane technology, a *head-up display* will project information onto the windshield. Instead of looking down at the dashboard, the driver can concentrate on the road ahead.

On the highway, computers will be able to measure the distance between the cars. You will automatically be kept at a safe distance from any vehicle or object.

In the future cars might drive themselves.

Sensors in the car of the future will be able to detect bumps and potholes in the road ahead, and adjust the suspension accordingly to give the smoothest possible ride.

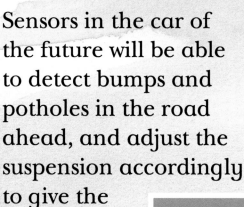

I didn't know that cars in the future will have brains. They will have a central computer that will control many of their functions. They will probably be similar in style to the "people carriers" seen around today.

Glossary

Aerodynamic
A shape, like a modern car, which cuts through air easily.

Airbag
A sack that fills with air when a car hits an object, it protects the driver and passengers.

Electric engine
An engine that is powered by electric energy stored in batteries. Electric engines do not produce waste products like those that burn gasoline or diesel.

Formula One
The set of rules describing car specifications that Formula One cars have to follow.

Gasoline engine
An engine that burns gasoline to move a car. Gasoline engines give off poisonous gases.

Head-up display
The projection of information

onto the cockpit of an airplane or the windshield of a car. The car drivers can then see it without taking their eyes off the road.

Mass-produced

Manufactured on a large scale using machines and people to carry out different parts of the construction process.

Production Line

A manufacturing method in which workers are positioned in lines. The work passes from stage to stage.

Road car

A car that is on sale to the public, used for driving on the roads instead of in races.

Solar panel

A device that collects energy from the sun's rays and turns it into electric energy for heating or driving an engine.

Sound barrier

Any vehicle that travels faster than sound waves move through the air (about 1083 feet per second at ground level) is said to have broken the sound barrier.

Suspension

A system of springs or other devices that smooth out the ride of a vehicle.

Index